YOUR KNOWLEDGE HA

Renu Rawat

Genome annotation and finding repetitive DNA elements

GRIN Verlag

Bibliografische Information der Deutschen Nationalbibliothek:

Die Deutsche Bibliothek verzeichnet diese Publikation in der Deutschen National-
bibliografie; detaillierte bibliografische Daten sind im Internet über http://dnb.d-
nb.de/ abrufbar.

Imprint:

Copyright © 2014 GRIN Verlag GmbH
Druck und Bindung: Books on Demand GmbH, Norderstedt Germany
ISBN: 978-3-656-65981-5

This book at GRIN:

http://www.grin.com/en/e-book/273971/genome-annotation-and-finding-repetitive-
dna-elements

ABSTRACT

As the number of genomes sequenced is increasing at high rate, there is a need of gene prediction method which is quick, reliable, and inexpensive. In such conditions, the computational tool will serve as an alternative to wet lab methods. The confidence level of annotation by the tool can be enhanced by preparing exhaustive training data sets. The aim is to develop a tool which will read data from a DNA sequence file in the fasta format and will annotate it. For this purpose Genome Database was used to retrieve the input data. PERL programming has been put to develop this tool for annotation. To increase the confidence level of annotation the data was validated from multiple sources. Perl script was written to find the promoter region, repeats, transcription factor binding site, base periodicity, and nucleotide frequency. The program written was also executed to identify repeats, poly (A) signals, CpG islands, ARS. The tool will annotate the DNA by predicting the gene structure based on the consensus sequences of important regulatory elements. The confidence level of annotation of the predicted gene, non-coding region, ARS, repeats etc. were checked by running test dataset. This test dataset was annotated data as reported by genome database and computational tools. Gene prediction of the non-coding regions as reported by genome database (SGD) were performed by existing tools; the regions identified as non-coding by these tools were then analyzed for presence of repeats. The BLAST was used to annotate on the basis of sequence similarity with the already annotated genes. GeneMark.hmm and FGENESH were used for gene prediction. In order to validate the predicted results, annotations of genome of Saccharomyces cerevisiae from SGD Database, and output of different computational tools viz, Emboss-CpGplot, PolyAh, REPFind, Promoter 2.0 Prediction Server were compared with the output of developed tool. The output generated was also used for validation and checking sensitivity of the tool. Such tools reduce the cost and time required for genome annotation and bridges the gap between sequenced and annotated data.

KEYWORDS

Genome Annotation, Gene structure, Gene prediction, Yeast genome, *Saccharomyces cerevisiae,* promoter recognition, Comparative genomics, computational tools, Bioinformatics.

INTRODUCTION

The hereditary material in the living cells is DNA. It is a large molecule made up of smaller units called nucleotides. Each nucleotide has three parts: a sugar molecule, a phosphate molecule, and a nitrogenous base. The genetic information is carried in the nitrogenous base. Nitrogenous bases are divided into two groups; purine and pyrimidine. This classification is based on the structural formulae. Pyrimidine has only one nitrogenized carbon ring and purines have two nitrogenized associated carbon rings. Cytosine, thymine and uracil are pyrimidine and adenine and guanine are purines. These bases are represented by their first letters, G, A, T and C. DNA is a double stranded molecule that forms helical structure. The two strands are complementary to each other whereby an A on one strand always binds to T and C always binds to G. DNA is associated with proteins to form chromosome.

Genome consists of complete content of genetic information in an organism. Eukaryotic genome is made up of a single, haploid set of chromosomes. The cell has two copies of these haploid set except reproductive and red blood cells. Genome Sequencing involves the determination of the order of nucleotides (A, T, G, and C) within a DNA molecule. Genome sequencing helps in numerous fields including biological research, diagnostic, biotechnology, forensic biology, evolutionary biology and biological systematics.

The literal meaning of annotation is to add explanation. And so, genome annotation is the process of attaching biological information to genomic sequences. Genome annotation helps in identification of important gene functions. The process of identification of genomic elements, intron-exon structure, coding regions, regulatory motifs comes under Structural genome annotation. The addition of biological information to these genomic elements referred as Functional genome annotation.

Genome annotation has led to the advancement in several fields like medicine, agriculture, biotechnology, chemistry and other basic science. Genome annotation is widely used in genetic engineering to develop genetic engineered crops (drought resistant, insect resistant) and genetically modified organisms (GMO). It is also used in Molecular medicine for better diagnosis of diseases, early detection of diseases, gene therapies etc. After genome annotation, the gene product of a particular sequence can be known and the biochemical functions can be established. Genome annotation is being used to reconstruct metabolic pathways e.g. the metabolic network in the yeast *Saccharomyces cerevisiae* was reconstructed using currently available genomic, biochemical, and physiological information. It also aids construction of transport reactions for transporter proteins based on genome annotation of an organism [1]. It plays role in food safety. If the genome of pathogen or the microorganisms responsible for food spoilage is annotated, the gene regulatory sequences can be found and thus the gene expression profile can be exploited to repress its growth and thereby increasing the shelf life of the food. It also helps in phylogenetic studies i.e. understanding the course of evolution. It has led to discoveries that are useful in energy production, toxic waste reduction and industrial processing.

Genome annotation consists of two phase; computation phase and annotation phase. In computation phase the genetic elements like intron, exon, protein, etc. are computed. This can either be done by, homology search or by prediction based methods. Homology search rely on sequence similarity search by aligning query to mRNA sequences (ESTs) and prediction based methods rely on the algorithms designed to find genes/gene structures based on nucleotide sequence and composition. The second phase is annotation phase which includes use of the computed data to synthesize gene annotation including functional annotation. Genome annotation pipeline starts with searching sequence databases (typically, NCBI NR) for sequence similarity, usually using BLAST. It is followed by statistical prediction of protein-coding genes using methods like GeneMark or Glimmer. The conserved domains are identified by specialized database search such as Pfam, SMART, and CDD, COGs. Functional predictions are refined using metabolic databases, such as KEGG [Fig. 1].

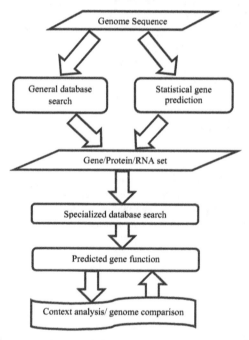

Fig 1: Flow chart of genome annotation process: FB: feedback from gene identification for correction of sequencing errors, primarily frameshifts. General database search: usually using

Genome annotation and finding repetitive DNA elements

BLAST. Statistical gene prediction: GeneMark or Glimmer. Specialized database search: Pfam, SMART, CDD, COGs. Functional prediction: metabolic databases such as KEGG.

Prokaryotes have high gene density (1 kb per gene on average); short intergenic regions and they lack introns. Unlike prokaryotes, Eukaryotes have split genes with high number of introns and exons, their gene density (1-200 kb per gene) is low and the non-coding regions have large sections of repeats. Hence, genome annotation is much easier in prokaryotes than eukaryotes [Fig.2].

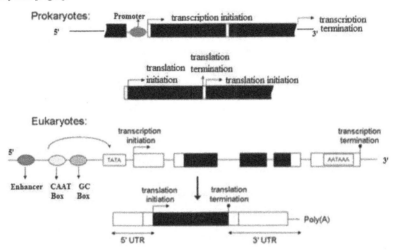

Fig 2: Schematic representation of prokaryotic and eukaryotic gene structure and transcription units. TATA denotes one of the possible eukaryotic core promoter elements, and poly (A) denotes the posttranscriptional addition of a poly (A) tail. Black bars denote coding DNA, open bars denote transcribed but untranslated DNA, and thin lines within transcribed regions denote introns. [2]

Table 1: Prokaryotic and eukaryotic genome organization

Prokaryotes	Eukaryotes
Prokaryotes have small genomes.	Eukaryotes have large genomes.
Prokaryotes have high gene density.	Eukaryotes have low gene density.
Prokaryotes rarely have introns (or splicing).	Eukaryotes have introns (splicing).
Prokaryotes do not have RNA processing.	Eukaryotes have RNA processing.
Prokaryotes have similar promoters.	Eukaryotes have heterogeneous promoters.

Prokaryotic terminators are important.	Eukaryotes terminators are not important.
Prokaryotes have overlapping genes.	Eukaryotes have polyadenylation.

The non-coding region has role in regulation of gene expression; these regulatory regions may also have repetitive elements. The repeats can be divided into two types; tandem repeats and dispersed repeats. When the pattern of one or more nucleotides is present as consecutive copies along a DNA strand it is called Tandem repeat e.g. satellite, minisatellite, and microsatellite. The repeats that are distributed throughout genomes are called Dispersed repeat sequences.

There are two approaches to predict gene; *ab-initio* [Fig: 3] and comparative. *Ab-initio* gene prediction is based on gene content and signal detection e.g. promoter and regulatory sequences that precede a gene, binding sites for the poly A tail at the end of a gene, CpG islands (stretches of DNA with high GC content). *Ab-initio* methods can easily predict novel genes but are not effective in detecting alternately spliced forms, interleaved or overlapping genes. They also have difficulty in accurate identification of exon/intron boundaries.

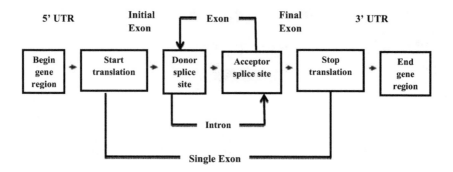

Fig 3: Flow chart of gene prediction process by HMM: Each box and arrow has associated *transition probabilities*, and *emission probabilities* for emission of nucleotides (dotted arrow). These are *learnt* from examples of known gene models and provide the probability that a stretch of sequence is a gene.

Comparative methods use annotations from previously analyzed genomes i.e. compare genomic sequence data to gene, cDNA, EST and protein sequences already present in databases. For the purpose of searching for genes in DNA sequences derived from eukaryotes, dbEST is particularly useful. This is a database of ESTs that have been generated by single pass sequencing of random clones from cDNA libraries. Genomic sequences are compared directly to the contents of dbEST in order to identify potential ORFs [3].

REVIEW OF LITERATURE

Many genome annotation pipelines and tools are available e.g. NCBI Eukaryotic Genome Annotation Pipeline [4], MAKER2 [5]. These pipelines use both or either of the two approaches *ab-initio* and comparative search. BLAST is used for comparative search. It identifies sequences similar to query from database such as GenBank or Swiss-Prot. EST sequence database contains all the transcripts. ESTs are DNA sequences of expressed genes that are represented in a cDNA library [6]. As they are derived from cDNA, then are transcribed from functioning gene. Therefore, the predicted genes are also used as a BLAST query against an EST database. BLASTN queries a nucleotide sequence against a nucleotide database, BLASTX translates a nucleotide query into all six frames and searches a protein database, and BLASTP uses a protein sequence to search a protein database [7].Numerous *ab initio* gene prediction methods have been developed [8].

Gene can be predicted using conserved regions of the genome. Regulatory elements like promoter sequences, polyadenylation signal, 5' capping signal can be used to predict gene. Promoter sequence is a region of DNA that initiates transcription of a particular gene. Promoters are located near the transcription start sites of genes, on the same strand and upstream on the DNA. Promoters can be about 100–1000 base pairs long. Eukaryotic promoters can contain a TATA element (consensus sequence TATAAA), and a BRE. The TATA element and BRE typically are located close to the transcriptional start site (typically within 30 to 40 base pairs). E-box (sequence CACGTG), are promoter regulatory sequences that binds to TFB proteins to regulate transcription. CAAT box or CAT box is a distinct pattern of nucleotides with GGCCAATCT consensus sequence that occur, 75-80 bases upstream to the initial transcription site. GC box has GGGCGG as consensus sequence. CAAT and GC are primarily located in the region from 100-150bp upstream from the TATA box. In *Saccharomyces cerevisiae* the TSS have been reported to be 45–120 bp downstream of a TATA element (9).

CAP site is transcription initiation sequence or start point defined as +1, at which the transcription process actually starts. The consensus sequence is ATG. Poly (A) signal with consensus AAUAAA is found 10-30nt upstream of the polyA site. When AATAAA is deleted from the DNA template, no mature mRNA is made requirement for both AAUAAA and GU or U-rich signals for efficient mature 3' end formation The AAUAAA signal is sufficient for polyadenylation if it is located at the appropriate distance from the end of a molecule. PolyA tails function in mRNA stabilization and in initiation of translation

Genome annotation and finding repetitive DNA elements

Analysis of the codon usage and base periodicity also help in gene annotation because they show marked differences between coding and non-coding regions [10]. Most of exon sequences have a 3-base periodicity, while intron sequences do not have this unique feature. This periodicity in exons is determined by codon usage frequencies [11]. The 3-base periodicity exists in many exon sequences due to the non-uniform distribution of the four nucleotides *A, C, T, G* in protein-coding region. Introns rather show 2-base periodicity. ORFs are expected to be shorter in DNA sequences with high AT (Adenine + Thymine) levels >50%. The reason is that A and T are more frequent in stop codons than G. Since there are three stop codons and 61 amino acid codons, (3:61) a stop codon occurs with a probability of approximately one in twenty (1:20). Furthermore, given three base pairs per codon, this should lead to one stop codon every sixty base pairs, in which A, C, G or T are equally likely to occur. The identification of segments with GC content much higher than average GC content, and a higher CpG frequency than average frequency of the CpG dinucleotide, could be indicative of a CpG island. Such islands are found at the 5' end. The frequency of stop codons may vary significantly depending upon the local nucleotide. So, it can be interpreted that the probability of an ORF being a coding sequence increases with its size. Most proteins are larger than 100 codons (300 bp) and their ORFs are relatively easy to classify. UTRs are sections of the mRNA before the start codon and after the stop codon that are not translated, termed the five prime untranslated region (5' UTR) and three prime untranslated region (3' UTR), respectively. These regions are transcribed with the coding region and thus are exonic as they are present in the mature mRNA. UTR has many roles in gene expression including mRNA stability, mRNA localization, and translational efficiency. UTRScan predicts functional elements by searching sequences for patterns located in 5' or 3' UTR sequences. DNA sequence can be examined to find sites for all restriction enzymes that cut the sequence. The recognition site of these restriction enzymes might be flanking the gene and thus would be important in the genetic engineering. A sequence-tagged site (or STS) is a short (200 to 500 base pair) DNA sequence that has a single occurrence in the genome and whose location and base sequence are known. STSs can be easily detected by the polymerase chain reaction (PCR) using specific primers. The DNA sequence of an STS may contain repetitive elements. Eukaryotic genomes are characterized and often dominated by repetitive, non-genic DNA sequences [12].

PERL, practical extraction and report language, is a high-level, general-purpose, interpreted, dynamic programming language. Perl was originally developed by Larry Wall in 1987 as a general-purpose UNIX scripting language to make report processing easier. The language provides powerful text processing facilities facilitating easy manipulation of text files. It is also used for graphics programming, system administration, network programming, applications that require database access and CGI programming on the Web.

The tool developed finds the coding region on the basis of presence of promoter region and transcription factor binding site. Majority of the non-coding region contains repetitive elements. The tool identifies repetitive DNA in the non-coding regions.

RATIONALE AND SCOPE OF PROJECT

This project aims to develop computational tool for genome annotation. There has been an exponential increase in the number of genomes sequenced in the past decade. Accurately predicting genes can significantly reduce the amount of experimental verification work which is time and labor consuming as well as expensive to carry out. *Ab initio* gene prediction plays a critical role because it predicts gene structures quickly, inexpensively, and in most cases reliably. The transcripts predicted by *ab initio* algorithms are normally complete and *ab initio* prediction results in at least partial prediction for about 95% of all genes, leaving fewer entirely missing genes [13].

SCOPE:

As the number of genomes sequenced is increasing at high rate, there is a need of gene prediction method which is quick, reliable, inexpensive. In such conditions, the tool provides will serve as an alternative to wet lab methods. The confidence level of annoation by the tool can be enhanced by preparing exhaustive training data sets.

RESEARCH METHODOLOGY

The project aims to develop a tool which will read a DNA sequence file (the fasta format) and will annotate it i.e. determine the important genomic elements including exon, intron, promoter region, identify repeats, TFBS, poly (A) signal, ARS, CpG islands, sequence tagged sites. For this purpose Perl programming will be implemented. The results of the program will be analyzed. The sensitivity of the tool can be validated by running on test dataset. This test dataset will be annotated data as reported by genome database and computational tools *viz.*, RepeatMasker [14], LTR_finder [15], tRNAScan-SE [16], UTRScan [17]. The transcription factor binding sites will be retrieved from YEASTRACT [18].

Genome annotation and finding repetitive DNA elements

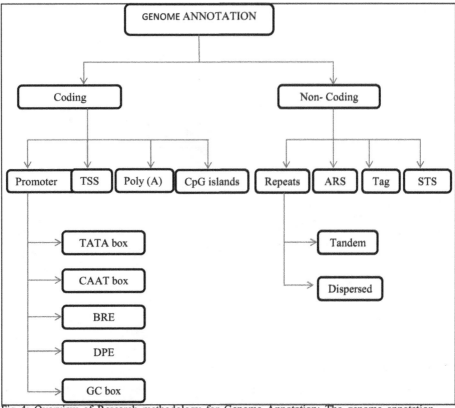

Fig 4: Overview of Research methodology for Genome Annotation: The genome annotation process can be divided into two parts, (a)predicting coding region, which can be predicted on the basis of promoter sequence, TSS, poly (A) signal; (b): non coding region mainly contain regulatory sequence and these regions can be predicted by searching for specific repeat, ARS, STS, Tag

Table 2: The consensus sequences of the conserved elements that were used for pattern search in the program

ELEMENT	CONSENSUS
TATABOX	TAT[AT][AT]A
CAAT BOX	GGCCAATCT

Genome annotation and finding repetitive DNA elements

GC BOX	GGGCGG
BRE	[GC][GC][GA]CGCC
INR	YYANWYY i.e. [CT][CT]A[ATGC][AT][CT][CT]
DPE	RGWYV[T] i.e. [AG]G[AT][CT][ACG]T
Poly (A)	AATAAA
ARS	[TA]TTTA[CT][AG]TTT[TA]
E BOX	CANNTG
5' Splice site	GTATGT
3' Splice site	[CT]AG
Branch point	TACTAAC
Donor Acceptor ss pair	GT.*AG or [CT]AGGT[AG]AGT.*[CT]{11}[ACGT][CT]AG[GA]

ALGORITHM

.

PROMOTER IDENTIFICATION

1. Input read from file (Fasta format) as specified by filename.
2. Store each line in an array element.
3. Remove the first line.
4. Open file in write mode to store output.
5. Store the consensus sequence of promoter in a scalar variable.
6. Concatenate first n elements of the DNA array, n is size of promoter consensus sequence. Store it in another scalar variable.
7. Initialize another variable with zero to count the occurrence of promoter.
8. Compare the two variables to find the presence of promoter sequence.
9. If match found, print the position in output file and increase the count by 1.
10. If no match found, slide the window by 1bp and then again concatenate next n elements and search for promoter sequence using string comparison.
11. Print the number of times promoter occurs.

Genome annotation and finding repetitive DNA elements

BASE PERIODICITY CALCULATION

1. Input read from file (Fasta format) as specified by filename.
2. Store each line in an array element.
3. Remove the first line.
4. 3-Base periodicity
   - Calculate the number of A, C, G, T present at third position for all the three frames.
   - Calculate the relative percentage of A, G, C and T at third position.
5. 2- Base periodicity
   - Calculate the number of A, C, G, T present at second position for all the three frames.
   - Calculate the relative percentage of A, G, C and T at third position.
6. Open file in write mode to store output.

REPEATS IDENTIFICATION

1. Input read from file (Fasta format) as specified by filename.
2. Store each line in an array element.
3. Remove the first line.
4. Open file in write mode to store output.
5. Ask user to define the range of repeat. i.e. minimum and maximum size of the repeat.
6. Concatenate first n elements, where, n is minimum size of repeat.
7. Store it in a scalar variable.
8. Search the DNA sequence for this pattern using string comparision.
9. If match found, print the position in output file.
10. If no match found, slide the window and thereby concatenate next n elements.
11. Repeat the steps till the end of the DNA sequence.
12. Concatenate first n+ 1 element, and repeats the step 7 to step 11.
13. Concatenate first n+1 element, and so on.
14. Repeat it till the concatenation of first m elements where m is the maximum size of repeat.

STS IDENTIFICATION

1. Input read from file (Fasta format) as specified by filename.
2. Store each line in an array element.
3. Remove the first line.
4. Join the array elements and store in a scalar variable, representing DNA sequence.

Genome annotation and finding repetitive DNA elements

5. Open file in write mode to store output.
6. Splice first 100nt from DNA sequence and store in another variable.
7. Now search the remaining DNA sequence for the presence of spliced 100nt using regular expression.
8. If match found, print the positions in the output file.
9. If match not found slide the window and again search for pattern match.
10. Repeat till the end of DNA sequence.

ARS IDENTIFICATION

1. Input read from file (Fasta format) as specified by filename.
2. Store each line in an array element.
3. Remove the first line.
4. Open file in write mode to store output.
5. Store the consensus sequence of ARS in a scalar variable.
6. Concatenate first n elements of the DNA array, n is size of ARS consensus sequence. Store it in another scalar variable.
7. Compare the two variables to find the presence of ARS.
8. If match found, print the position in output file.
9. If no match found, slide the window by 1bp and then again concatenate next n elements and search for promoter sequence using string comparison.

NUCLEOTIDE FREQUENCY CALCULATION

1. Input read from file (Fasta format) as specified by filename.
2. Store each line in an array element.
3. Remove the first line.
4. Open file in write mode to store output.
5. Calculate the number of A, G, C and T present in the DNA.
   - Take four variables to count A, G, C and T respectively.
   - Initialize them with zero.
   - Compare each element of the array with A, C, G and T.
   - Increase the count by 1 of that nucleotide to which it matches.
   - Repeat the steps till the end of the DNA sequence.
6. Calculate relative percentage of AT and GC.

TFBS IDENTIFICATION

Genome annotation and finding repetitive DNA elements

1. Input read from file (Fasta format) as specified by filename.
2. Store each line in an array element.
3. Remove the first line.
4. Join the array elements and store in a scalar variable.
5. Input read Transcription factor binding site data from file as specified by filename.
6. Store each line in an array element.
7. Open file in write mode to store output.
8. Search for the element of tfbs array along the DNA sequence using regular expression.
9. If pattern match found, print the positions in output file.
10. If pattern not found search for the next array element.
11. Repeat the process for all elements of the array.

TAG IDENTIFICATION

1. Input read from file (Fasta format) as specified by filename.
2. Store each line in an array element.
3. Remove the first line.
4. Join the array elements and store in a scalar variable.
5. Input read Tag data from file as specified by filename.
6. Store each line in an array element.
7. Open file in write mode to store output.
8. Search the first element of tag array along the DNA sequence using regular expression.
9. If pattern match found, print the positions in output file.
10. If pattern not found search for the next array element.
11. Repeat the process for all elements of the array.

Genome annotation and finding repetitive DNA elements

POLYADENYLATION IDENTIFICATION
1. Input read from file (Fasta format) as specified by filename.
2. Store each line in an array element.
3. Remove the first line.
4. Open file in write mode to store output.
5. Concatenate first n elements of the DNA array, n is size of poly (A) consensus sequence. Store it in another scalar variable.
6. Compare the two variables to find the presence of poly (A) signal.
7. If match found, print the position in output file.
8. If no match found, slide the window by 1bp and then again concatenate next n elements and search for poly (A) signal using string comparison.

CpG_ISLAND IDENTIFICATION

1. Input read from file (Fasta format) as specified by filename.
2. Store each line in an array element.
3. Remove the first line.
4. Join the array elements and store in a scalar variable that represent DNA sequence.
5. Open file in write mode to store output.
6. For first window i.e. first 200nt number of C's, G's and CpG's are computed
7. The respective percentage and ratio are calculated.
8. For the next position i, the previous position (i-1) and the last position in the window are added or subtracted to the previous number of C's, G's and CpG's.
9. Then percentage and ratio are calculated to each position.
10. When a position has both percentage and ratio higher than their thresholds 55% and 0.65, respectively, it is assigned as an island start position.
11. The following position with values lower than the thresholds is determined as final position.
12. The distance between initial and final positions is calculated.
13. Only the islands longer than 200nt are considered [19, 20].

RESEARCH AND EXPERIMENTAL WORK DONE

The genomic sequence of *Saccharomyces cerevisiae* S288c was retrieved from the Genome Database of NCBI. The Genome database contains sequence and map data of genomes of over 1000 species or strains. These represent both completely sequenced genomes and draft genome [21].

Perl script was written to annotate the regions not reported as coding. Perl program was written that reads data from file (Fasta format) and detects the presence of Promoter region. The consensus sequences of TATA-box, GC-box, and CAAT-box were used to locate the promoter region. Another program that calculates relative frequency of nucleotide in the sequence i.e. A, G, C, T, AG% and GC% was written. Similarly programs for 3-base periodicity and 2- base periodicity were written. The program to identify CpG islands was written. Validate the locus of CpG islands Emboss-cpgplot can be used. Perl program was generated which translate the DNA sequence and then save it in a file.

After gene prediction a dataset was created that included all the information about coding and non-coding regions, hypothetical proteins, RNA coding genes, additional features like autonomously replicating sequences, repetitive DNA elements

RESULTS AND DISCUSSION

The tool was successfully made. This tool reads a file and successfully finds promoter region, repetitive elements, transcription binding sites, nucleotide frequency, autonomously replicating sequences, sequence tagged sites. To check the confidence level of the genome annotation by this tool, pre-annotated genome of *Saccharomyces cerevisiae* is retrieved form SGD and validated using this tool. Using Perl programing the result was saved in file.

Table 3: ARS signal predicted by tool: the genomic sequence of chromosome was retrieved from Genbank and using pattern match with its consensus sequence following no of ARS were predicted by the tool.

Accession No.	Chr	Predicted ARS (No.)	Region
NC_001133.9	I	6	650..1791, 70257..70489, 124349..124597, 159907..160127, 176157..176404
NC_001134.8	II	7	170088..170336, 254206..255370, 326140..326375, 407876..408108, 622671..622939, 631939..632251, 792164..792388
NC_001135.5	III	4	14871..15213, 108780..109295, 292388..292921
NC_001136.10	IV	6	137..1392, 212420..212668, 483852..484096, 505343..505584, 567496..567742, 1109964..1110204
NC_001137.3	V	5	6464..7230, 173638..173875, 287507..287752, 498422..499348, 569025..570090
NC_001138.5	VI	3	118637..118957, 256277..256431, 269417..270035
NC_001139.9	VII	6	203914..204155, 484930..485157, 568490..568737, 574622..574915, 659809..660053, 977728..977976
NC_001140.6	VIII	3	7536..7783, 447622..447855, 556001..556331.
NC_001141.2	IX	3	175038..175358, 214679..214922, 357160..357396
NC_001142.9	X	4	65..577, 228552..229043, 337281..337529

Genome annotation and finding repetitive DNA elements

Table 4: TFBS signal predicted by tool: the genomic sequence of chromosome was retrieved from Genbank and the TFBS were extracted from YEASTRACT. Using pattern match with its consensus sequence following no of TFBS were predicted by the tool.

Accession No.	Chromosome	TFBS
NC_001133.9	I	180
NC_001134.8	II	205
NC_001135.5	III	198
NC_001136.10	IV	212
NC_001137.3	V	196
NC_001138.5	VI	186
NC_001139.9	VII	201

Table 5: TATA box signal predicted by tool: the genomic sequence of chromosome was retrieved from Genbank and using pattern match with its consensus sequence following no of TATABOX were predicted by the tool.

Accession No.	Chr	TATABOX
NC_001133.9	I	411
NC_001134.8	II	1650
NC_001135.5	III	649
NC_001136.10	IV	3312
NC_001137.3	V	1246
NC_001138.5	VI	542
NC_001139.9	VII	2363

Genome annotation and finding repetitive DNA elements

Table 6: Tag sequence predicted by tool: the genomic sequence of chromosome was retrieved from Genbank and following no of Tag sequence elements were predicted by the tool.

Accession No.	Chr	TAG seq
NC_001133.9	I	85
NC_001134.8	II	300
NC_001135.5	III	71
NC_001136.10	IV	609
NC_001137.3	V	267
NC_001138.5	VI	63
NC_001139.9	VII	343

Table 7: CpG islands predicted by tool: the genomic sequence of chromosome was retrieved from Genbank and the following data were predicted by the tool.

Accession No.	Chr	CpG islands		Region	Length	CG%
NC_001133.9	I	3	1	190402..191304	902	58.76%
			2	191483..191702	219	56.16%
			3	191811..192064	253	58.89%
NC_001136.10	IV	1	1	893983..894215	232	56.47%
NC_001137.3	V	3	1	191916..192218	302	55.30%
			2	335479..335689	210	56.67%
			3	441979..442250	271	55.72%
NC_001138.5	VI	1	1	224844..225307	463	58.53%

Genome annotation and finding repetitive DNA elements

			1	271331..271533	202	54.95%
NC_001139.9	VII	3	2	271597..271982	385	58.70%
			3	625145..625438	293	58.02%
NC_001140.6	VIII	2	1	175986..176192	206	55.83%
			2	189297..189512	215	55.81%
NC_001141.2	IX	2	1	53302..53531	229	56.33%
			2	53955..54255	300	56.33%
NC_001142.9	X	1	1	639355..639570	215	56.74%
NC_001143.9	XI	2	1	68180..68461	281	56.58%
			2	278288..278506	218	56.88%
NC_001144.5	XII	2	1	423884..424374	490	58.98%
			2	489391..489630	239	57.32%
NC_001145.3	XIII	1	1	408142..408408	266	54.14%
NC_001146.8	XIV	2	1	198447..198811	364	57.14%
			2	349906..350154	248	54.84%
NC_001147.6	XV	4	1	109263..109565	302	57.95%
			2	480063..480298	235	57.02%
			3	480739..480992	253	55.73%
			4	988165..988405	240	55.42%
NC_001148.4	XVI	1	1	645359..645577	218	56.42%

Genome annotation and finding repetitive DNA elements

Table 8: Poly (A) signal predicted by tool: the genomic sequence of chromosome was retrieved from Genbank and following no of Poly (A) signals were predicted by the tool by pattern match using its consensus sequence.

Accession No.	Chr	Poly(A) signal
NC_001133.9	I	980
NC_001134.8	II	1096
NC_001135.5	III	772
NC_001136.10	IV	942
NC_001137.3	V	772
NC_001138.5	VI	672
NC_001139.9	VII	761
NC_001140.6	VIII	419
NC_001141.2	IX	562
NC_001142.9	X	1140
NC_001143.9	XI	242
NC_001144.5	XII	560
NC_001145.3	XIII	1581
NC_001146.8	XIV	334
NC_001147.6	XV	835
NC_001148.4	XVI	222
NC_001224.1	mt	793

Table 9: DPE signal predicted by tool: the genomic sequence of chromosome was retrieved from Genbank and following no of DPE elements were predicted by the tool.

Accession No.	Chr	DPE
NC_001133.9	I	1324
NC_001134.8	II	4340
NC_001135.5	III	1654
NC_001136.10	IV	8303
NC_001137.3	V	3173
NC_001138.5	VI	1470
NC_001139.9	VII	5916
NC_001140.6	VIII	3033
NC_001141.2	IX	2355
NC_001142.9	X	4082
NC_001143.9	XI	3569
NC_001144.5	XII	5890
NC_001145.3	XIII	4981
NC_001146.8	XIV	4253
NC_001147.6	XV	5886
NC_001148.4	XVI	5187
NC_001224.1	mt	323

VALIDATION

The validation of predictions was done by matching predicted gene to previously annotated cDNA, matching to EST from same organism, similarity of nucleotide or conceptually translated protein sequence to sequences in GenBank. Furthermore, predicted gene was validated by confirming the presence of associated regulatory sequences like promoter sequences, i.e. TATA box; CpG islands, by calculating its nucleotide content. Usually, coding regions have higher GC% than non-coding region. The GC-content of Yeast (*Saccharomyces cerevisiae*) is 38%

In order to validate the predicted results, annotations of genome of *Saccharomyces cerevisiae* from SGD Database were compared with the tool output [22]. To validate the predicted CpG islands the output of the tool is compared with the output of the Emboss-CpGplot tool [23]. Similarly, to validate predicted poly (A) signals the output of the tool is compared with the output of the PolyAh tool [24]. To validate the predicted repetitive elements, the output of the tool is compared with the output of the REPFind and REPuter tool [25, 26]. To validate the predicted promoter region, the output of the tool is compared with the annotation of *Saccharomyces cerevisiae* from SGD database and the output of Promoter 2.0 Prediction Server [27].

Table 10: ARS predicted as output of developed tool and extracted by SGD

Accession No.	Chr	ARS predicted by tool	ARS extracted from SGD
NC_001133.9	I	650..1791	650..1791
		17149..17160	7997..8547
		124349..124597	30946..31183
		159907..160127	41808..42182
		171816..171827	70257..70489
		176157..176404	124349..124597
		208605..208616	159907..160127

Genome annotation and finding repetitive DNA elements

		229450..229461	176157..176404
NC_001134.8	II	53415..53426 122598..122609 170088..170336 189470..189481 195767..195778 254206..255370 326140..326375 368745..368756 381151..381162 407876..408108 420235..420246 622671..622939 631939..632251 665038..665049 792164..792388	28942..29160 6319..63427 170088..170336 198232..198472 237684..237918 254206..255370 326140..326375 407876..408108 417784..418079 486707..486954 622671..622939 631939..632251 704296..704566 741558..741847 757437..757667 792164..792388
NC_001135.5	III	11256..11267 14871..15213 52343..52354 74520..74531 108780..109295 233373..233384 292388..292921	838..1551 14871..15213 15214..16274 30200..30657 108780..109295 114321..114939 131985..132328

Genome annotation and finding repetitive DNA elements

		315820..315831	292388..292921

Table 11: Poly (A) signal predicted as output of developed tool and by POLYAH tool, Accession no. NC_001224.1

137	137
323	323
2925	2925
3336	3336
9898	9898
10059	10059
9898	9898
19992	19992
	20244
23916	23916
23977	23977
24189	24189
24363	
25636	25636
26132	
27023	27023
	30315
30382	30382
	34061
49437	49437

Genome annotation and finding repetitive DNA elements

	56069
67691	67691
67775	67775
	67829
70090	70079
73408	
85695	

Table 12: Repetitive element predicted as output of developed tool and by REPFIND tool, Accession no. NC_001224.1

Repeat length	Tool	REPFind
14	1738, 37254	1738, 37254
	1804, 176652	1804, 176652
	1988, 65843	1872, 176720
	2081, 176929	1988, 65843
	6735, 23711, 101280, 192550	11874, 11901, 24306, 24333
	204657, 204792, 204927, 205062, 205332, 205467, 205602	204657, 204792, 204927, 205062, 205332, 205467, 205602
	23238, 45633, 69827, 126879, 152104, 199907, 223126	6735, 23711, 101280, 192550
15	1946, 176794	5789, 84600
	11689, 24121,	1946, 176794
	11874, 11901, 24306, 24333	11689, 24121,
	75000, 223150, 226918	11874, 11901, 24306, 24333
	45636, 74999, 223149, 226917	45636, 74999, 223149, 226917

16	12570, 12714, 24975	12570, 12714, 24975
	23236, 45631, 69825, 126877 152102, 223124	23236, 45631, 69825, 126877
		11874, 11901, 24306, 24333
	11874, 11901, 24306, 24333	
		204393, 204528, 204663, 204798
	204393, 204528, 204663, 204798	
		25677, 25812, 25947, 26082,
	25677, 25812, 25947, 26082, 26217	26217, 26352, 26487, 26622,
	26352, 26487, 26622, 26757, 27027	26757, 27027
17	11685, 24117	31120, 31502, 169225
	26169, 26844 26979	11685, 24117
	11874, 11901, 24306, 24333	11874, 11901, 24306, 24333
	45632, 69826, 126878, 152103 223125	45632, 69826, 126878, 152103 223125
	25716, 25851, 25986, 26121, 26256 26391, 27066	25584, 25719, 25854, 25989, 26124, 26259, 26394, 27069
18	26551, 26686 , 26821 , 26956	26551, 26686 , 26821 , 26956
	6735, 23711, 101280	6735, 23711, 101280
	11693 , 24125	11700 , 24132
	12276 , 24729	12276 , 24729
	26535, 26670, 26805, 26940	26535, 26670, 26805, 26940

Sensitivity = (TP / (TP+FN))

Specificity = (TN / (TN+FP))

Sn and Sp can have values in-between 0 and 1; with perfect prediction occurring only when both measures are equal to 1. Each of these measures is not sufficient by itself because perfect Sn can be obtained if all the nucleotides that are actual positives are correctly predicted as positives and perfect Sn if all the nucleotides that are actual negatives are correctly predicted as negatives. A single measure that captures both Sn and Sp called the correlation coefficient (CC) is defined as:

Genome annotation and finding repetitive DNA elements

$$CC = (TP*TN-FP*FN) / sqrt (TP+FP*TP+FN*TN+FP*TN+FN)$$

Table 13: Measuring predictive accuracy

	ARS	Promoter	Repeats	TFBS	CpG islands	DPE element	PolyA signal	Tag sites
TP	380	819	8891	1385	30	737	789	2154
TN	52	353	9500	1877	5	1256	779	2239
FP	80	937	29	963	41	912	4	37
FN	18	512	12	184	18	415	12	415
Sn	0.95	0.62	0.99	0.88	0.63	0.63	0.98	0.83
Sp	0.39	0.73	0.99	0.66	0.89	0.57	0.99	0.97
CC	0.44	0.34	0.98	0.52	0.53	0.21	0.97	0.82
SMC	0.81	0.45	0.99	0.74	0.37	0.60	0.98	0.90

CC measures the probability of a NT being predicted as positive given that it actually is positive and being predicted as negative given that it actually is negative. It ranges from 1 to -1. The higher the coefficient, more efficient is the developed tool; the lower the coefficient, less efficient is developed tool. The major flaw in the utility of CC is that it is undefined when any of the values on the denominator is equal to 0. That is, when, either reality or prediction lacks both positive and negative donor splice sites. To circumvent this problem, the SMC can be used, where

$$SMC = TP+TN / (TP+TN+FP+FN)$$

SMC is the measure of the probability that a given NT is correctly predicted, i.e., that it is assigned the same value (positive or negative) in both reality and prediction.

CONCLUSION

The tool developed focused on development of collection of PERL scripts for annotation of genome based on multiple features. The output generated was also used for validation and checking sensitivity of the tool. Such tools reduce the cost and time required for genome annotation and bridge the gap between sequenced and annotated data.

LIST OF ABBREVIATIONS

A	Adenine
ARS	Autonomously replicating sequence
BLAST	Basic local alignment search tool
BRE	B recognition element
CAAT	Consensus sequence is GGCCAATCT
cDNA	complementary DNA
C	Cytosine
CC	Correlation coefficient
CpG	—C—phosphate—G—
DNA	Deoxy ribonucleic acid
E-box	Consensus sequence CACGTG
EST	Expressed sequence tags
FP	False positive
FN	False negative
GC Box	Consensus sequence is GGGCGG
G	Guanine
INR	transcription initiator having consensus sequence YYANWYY
LTR	Long Terminal Repeat
mRNA	Messenger RNA
NT or nt	Nucleotide
ORF	Open reading frame

RNA	Ribonucleic acid
rRNA	Ribosomal RNA
STS	Sequence-tagged site
Sn	Sensitivity
SGD	*Saccharomyces* Genome Database
SMC	Simple matching coefficient
Sp	Specificity
T	Thymine
TATA	Consensus sequence is TAT[AT][AT]A
TFBS	Transcription factor
TFBS	Transcription factor binding sequence
TP	True positive
TN	True negative
tRNA	Transfer RNA
TSS	Transcription start site
UTR	UnTranslated region
U	Uracil

GLOSSARY

ARS	A portion of a split gene that is transcribed into RNA, but subsequently removed from within the transcript prior to translation
Exon	Exons are parts of DNA that are converted into mature messenger RNA (mRNA).
Gene	a specific sequence of nucleotides in DNA or RNA corresponding to a unit of inheritance, which is associated with regulatory regions, transcribed regions, and or other functional sequence regions
Intron	Introns are noncoding sections of an RNA transcript, or the DNA encoding it, that are spliced out before the RNA molecule is translated into a protein.
LTR	Identical sequences, typically several hundred nucleotides in length, that are located both at the ends of intact Ty retro transposons and as solo elements present in multiple copies throughout the genome. There are several types of LTR elements in yeast: delta, tau, sigma and omega
ORF	'ORF' refers to a stretch of DNA that could potentially be translated into a polypeptide or RNA: i.e., it begins with an ATG "start" codon and terminates with one of the 3 "stop" codons.
Transcription	DNA transcription is a process that involves transcribing genetic information from DNA to RNA
TP	The number of NTs which are both predicted positives and actual positive
FP	The number of NTs which are predicted positives but are actual negative
TN	The number of NTs which are both predicted negatives and actual positive

Genome annotation and finding repetitive DNA elements

FN   The number of NTs which are predicted negatives but are actual
                            positive

Sensitivity   Measures the proportion of actual positives which are correctly
                               identified. It is also called as the true positive rate.

Specificity   Measures the proportion of actual negatives which are correctly
                               identified. It is also called as the true negative rate.

ACKNOWLEDGEMENTS

I extend my utmost gratitude to my mentor Mrs. **Nishtha Pandey**, **Assistant Professor**, school of biotechnology, Lovely professional university, for giving me courage to bring this project and has encouraged me to get into more and more ventures. Continuing the same, she has provided me with many insights and useful examples, which proved to be of immense help in successful completion of this project. I cordially express my thankfulness and best regards to her for giving me the opportunity to undertake the project under her mentorship.

Finally, yet importantly, I would like to express my heartfelt thanks to my beloved parents for their blessings, my friends/classmates for their help for useful information and suggestions and wishes for the successful completion of this project. I am thankful to all for being very supportive in my endeavor during times of stress and for being the constant source of inspiration encouragement.

REFERENCES

1. Leel Thomas *et al*, "Annotation-based inference of transporter functions", *(Bioinformatics) Oxford Journals*, 24(13), 259-267.
2. Lynch Michael, "The origins of eukaryotic gene structure", *Molecular Biology and Evolution*, 2006, 23, 450-468.
3. Jiang J, Jacob HJ, "dbest: An automated tool using expressed sequence tags to delineate gene structure", *Genome Research*, 1998, 8, 268-275.
4. Angiuoli SV *et al*, "Toward an online repository of standard operating procedures (SOPs) for (meta) genomic annotation", *OMICS*, 2008, 12(2):137-41.
5. Holt C, Yandell M, "MAKER2: an annotation pipeline and genome-database management tool for second-generation genome projects", *BMC Bioinformatics*. 2011; 12:491
6. Boguski MS, Lowe TM, Tolstoshev CM, "dbEST — database for "expressed sequence tags", *Nature Genetics*, 1993, 4, 332 – 333.
7. Altschul SF *et al*, "Basic Local Alignment Search Tool", *J Mol Biol*, 1990, 215, 403-410.
8. Zhang, M.Q, "Computational prediction of eukaryotic protein-coding genes", *Nature Reviews Genetics*, 2002, 3, 698-709.
9. Hampsey M., "Molecular genetics of the RNA polymerase II general transcriptional machinery. Microbiol", *Mol. Biol. Rev.*, 1998, 62, 465–503.
10. Changchuan Yin, Stephen S.-T. Yau, "Prediction of protein coding regions by the 3-base periodicity analysis of a DNA sequence", *Science Direct, Journal Of Theoretical Biology* 2007, 247, 687-694
11. Eskesen Stephen, "Periodicity of DNA in exons", *Bmc Molecular Biology*, 2004, 5, 5-12.
12. Britten RJ, Kohne DE, "Repeated Sequences In DNA", *Science*, 1968, 161, 529–540
13. Li Jun, "Anopheles gambiae genome reannotation through synthesis of *ab initio* and comparative gene prediction algorithms", *Genome Biology*, 2006; 7(3): 24.
14. Tempel Sebastien, "Using and understanding RepeatMasker", *Methods in Molecular Biology*, 2012, 29-51.
15. Zhao Xu, Hao Wang, "LTR_FINDER: An efficient tool for the prediction of full-length LTR Retrotransposons", *Nucleic Acids Res.*, 2007, 35, 265-268.
16. Lowe Todd and Eddy Sean, "tRNAscan-SE: A program for improved detection of transfer RNA genes in genomic sequence", *Nucl. Acids Res.*, 1997, 25(5), 955-964.
17. Pesole G. and Liuni,S. "Internet resources for the functional analysis of 5′ and 3′ untranslated regions of eukaryotic mRNA", *Trends Genetics*, 1999, 15, 378

18. Teixeira C. Miguel *et al,* "The YEASTRACT database: a tool for the analysis of transcription regulatory associations in *Saccharomyces cerevisiae*", *Nucl. Acids Res.,* 34(1), 446-451.
19. Pereira Mariana, *et al,* "CpG island predictor", Bioinformatics and systems biology programme, Chalmers University of Technology, Goteborg Sweden.
20. Takai, D. and Jones, P. A., "Comprehensive analysis of CpG islands in human chromosomes 21 and 22", *Proc. Natl. Acad. Sci. USA,* 2002, 99, 3740-3745.
21. Mardis Elaine, McPherson John *et al;* "What is Finished, and Why Does it Matter", *Genome Research,* 2002, 12, 669-671
22. Cherry J. Michael *et al,* "*Saccharomyces* Genome Database: the genomics resource of budding yeast", *Nucleic Acids Res,* 2012, 700-705
23. McWilliam H, *et al* "Analysis tool web services from the EMBL-EBI", *Nucleic acids research,* 2013, 41, 597-600
24. Salamov A.A., Solovyev V.V. "Recognition of 3'-end cleavage and polyadenilation region of human mRNA precursors", *CABIOS,* 1997, 13 (1), 23-28.
25. http://zlab.bu.edu/repfind/ (ZLAB, Dr. Zhiping Weng, Boston University, U.S.A)
26. S. Kurtz *et al,* "REPuter: the manifold applications of repeat analysis on a genomic scale.", *Nucleic acids research,* 29 (22), 4633–4642
27. Steen Knudsen, "Promoter 2.0: for the recognition of PolII promoter sequences", *Bioinformatics,* 1999, 15, 356-361.
28. Lukashin AV, Borodovsky, "Genemark.Hmm: New Solutions for Gene Finding" *Nucleic Acids Res* 1998, 26, 1107-1115.
29. Eddy SR , "Noncoding RNA Genes", *Curr Opin Genet Dev* 1999, 9, 695-699.
30. Stein, L, "Genome Annotation: From Sequence To Biology" , *Nature Reviews Genetics* 2, 7, 2001, 493–503
31. Solovyev V, Kosarev P, Seledsov I, Vorobyev D, "Automatic Annotation Of Eukaryotic Genes", Pseudogenes And Promoters, *Genome Biol* 2006,7, Suppl 1: P. 10.1-10.12.
32. Yang, C, Bolotin, E, *et al,* " Prevalence Of The Initiator Over The TATA Box In Human And Yeast Genes And Identification Of DNA Motifs Enriched In Human TATA-Less Core Promoters" (2007), *Gene* 389 1 52–65.
33. Patricia Chisamore-Robert, "Directional Telomeric Silencing And Lack Of Canonical B1 Elements In Two Silencer Autonomously Replicating Sequences In *S. Cerevisiae",* *Bmc Molecular Biology* 2012, 13:34
34. Danchin EGJ, Levasseur A, Rascol VL, Gouret P, Pontarotti P, "The Use Of Evolutionary Biology Concepts For Genome Annotation", (2007), *Journal Of Experimental Zoology (Molecular Development And Evolution),* 308B, 26–36.
35. Jochen Förster *et al,* "Genome-scale reconstruction of the S*accharomyces cerevisiae* metabolic network", *Genome Research,* 2003, 13, 244-253

www.ingramcontent.com/pod-product-compliance
Lightning Source LLC
La Vergne TN
LVHW042303060326
832902LV00009B/1236